ZC HORSES
CHICKADEE THE TRAVELER

Diane W. Keaster

illustrated by Debbie Page

ISBN 0-9721496-7-8
ISBN 978-0-9721496-7-9

Printed in U.S.A.

ZC HORSES
CHICKADEE THE TRAVELER

To my brother Steve who has carried me through many bogs in my life.

ZC HORSES
SERIES

Be part of them all!

Chick - The Beginning!

Chick - The Saddle Horse!

Chick - The Mom!

Luke - The First!

Barbie - The Best!

Leroy - The Stallion!

And Many More!

ZC HORSES

CHICKADEE

THE TRAVELER

TABLE OF CONTENTS

1

GENERATIONS

Ranch life is a wonderful life. A ranch or the ranching profession may be handed down from generation to generation. In other words, a ranching father teaches his son to ranch. The son, then, teaches his son to ranch. So ranching is passed down to each generation. A generation means all the people born around the same time.

Many times, several past relatives chose the ranching profession.

That is how it was for me. My mother's grandfather was a rancher. That was Grandpa Rush. My father's two grandfathers ranched. They were Grandpa Keaster and Grandpa Murphy.

Grandpa Murphy's family was well-known. They were also extremely wealthy land owners in the eastern part of the United States. Along with the end of the Civil War, the family lost their wealth.

Like with Grandpa Keaster, the flowing Missouri River provided Grandpa Murphy transportation. He also landed in Fort Benton, Montana. This was his first experience with ranching in the West.

The first place he settled with his family was in the Highwood Mountains. This was where Grandpa Keaster ranched.

Grandpa Murphy later wanted to find what he felt was a better place to live. He went exploring the undeveloped Montana. He traveled over the Continental Divide. Where he crossed the divide is now Glacier National Park. Passing the stunning Flathead Lake, he traveled down the area we now know as the Swan Valley. This is along the edge of the Bob Marshall Wilderness. A wilderness is an immense area where no one lives.

Grandpa Murphy eventually found

one of the most beautiful areas in Montana. The great Rocky Mountains were his back yard. Green, lush meadows begged him to make this area his home. This area is now called Ovando. It was here that my brother Steve packed me on his shoulders through a bog to see the Murphy's buffalo. I was very young then.

Grandpa Murphy's family joined him at their new homestead. A

homestead is a piece of ground given by the government to a settler. He had sons and daughters. My grandmother, my father's mother, was one of those daughters.

All of Grandpa Murphy's children were involved with cattle and horses when they grew up. They even went to the Highwood Mountains, Grandpa Keaster's area, to buy bulls. A bull is the father of calves, baby cows.

The Bob Marshall Wilderness continually called to the Murphy family. It rested in sight of the ranch. The draw was so strong, one of the Murphys became the first outfitter in this massive wilderness. An outfitter is someone that takes people into an area camping. The outfitter provides the food, horses and camping equipment. My brothers continue to make a yearly trek into this wilderness.

A deep love for horses was in the hearts of all of Grandpa Murphy's children. Their love for horses

was passed down to their children. This would have been my father's generation. In turn, my father's generation passed this deep love down to their children. This was my generation. I, then, have passed this love down to my sons.

Just like with humans, horses have generations. Chick had many wonderful children. These children brought me much joy. Each had their own personality and special quality.

One had a quality quite special!

2
THE SIBLING

Chick and Dan had already had two wonderful foals, or babies, together. I was so thankful I had found both of them. Chick was a palomino, or golden colored. Dan was a gray. As mother and father, they had given me a gray filly, or girl, and a palomino. These two sisters were Barbie and Goldie. Since they had the same mother and father, they were considered 'full-sisters'.

How fun to see the color of a third foal out of these two. This would be a full-brother or sister to Barbie and Goldie. I was certain the foal would be palomino or gray. How could it be anything else?!

The eleven-month wait for the foal seemed like two years. Chick spent most of the time overlooking the deep Belt Valley. The hillside where she stood was covered with springs. This meant water oozed right out of the ground. The area where the cold water appeared was covered by a soft, green carpet of grass. Willows, leafy trees, shot up around it, too.

Belt Creek slithered below like a snake. It peeked out of its cushion of trees. Thimble-shaped Belt Butte watched Chick's every move.

Near the foaling date, April 25, Chick came home. She enjoyed basking in the warm Spring sun. The long branches of willow trees gave her shade when she needed it. Barbie and Goldie were always close at hand. They were excited to meet their new brother or sister.

Like always, I checked on Chick continually. Her belly looked like she swallowed a hot air balloon.

I had left the house for a while. It was April 24. I teased myself that Chick might have a black foal. I had always wanted one.

I was not gone long. It was a relief to be home again. I glanced at Chick. Her golden coat glistened in the sun. Robins were chirping their Spring song. There was a dark spot beside her. I figured I was imagining things since I had always wanted a black foal. The black spot would not leave my mind. I had to go see.

Rushing out to Chick's pen, I almost tripped. Amazement choked me. There, trotting beside its mom, was a beautiful coal-black foal. It did not have a speck of white on it. I could hardly believe this was Chick's baby! Chick's stomach was slender now.

This foal was a filly. She held her

head high in the air. Her trot was more like a prance. I hollered out, "Come here my little chickadee!" She stopped her prance and walked right to me. And what a walk she had! Dust rose behind her tiny feet. Not many big horses walk as fast and proud as the filly.

From then on she was dubbed Chickadee. Her registered name was Chickadee Bar Dial.

Hiding in Chickadee's soft, furry coat were a few gray hairs. This told me she was really a gray. A gray horse is always dark when it is first born. The horse's coat then turns lighter as the horse ages.

My heart was filled with joy! Chickadee came right up to me and was friendly.

Handling her was a different story!

3

THE ADOPTED MOM

Spunky Barbie had been terrible to halter break. She bucked in my arms when I tried to hold her. Holding a foal when it is born helps to get them used to people. Mild-mannered Goldie, though, was very nice to halter break and handle. She never gave me any trouble. I was anxious to see Chickadee's reaction. She was friendly and interested in me. I hoped she was even-tempered.

Chickadee strutted to me. I put one arm around her hind end and one around her chest. She was a soft fur ball in my arms. She blew up bucking. She had me bouncing like a rubber ball. Up and down we went. She was worse than Barbie! It took a lot to settle her down. I finally got the little blue halter on her that Luke, Barbie and Goldie had worn.

I did not know what to expect when I halter broke her. You are teaching a foal to lead when you halter break it. Chickadee needed to learn to lead. All horses do.

I attached the lead rope to Chickadee's halter. A lead rope is like a leash for a dog. Back she flew. She was up in the air. She was sideways. Once she even fell to the ground. I had to hold on to the lead rope with all my might. The whole time Chickadee was bellering like a cow. “Maaaaam, Maaaam,” she was crying. She hoped Chick would come to her rescue.

Chick knew Chickadee had to learn to lead. She was concerned, though. Every so often a caring nicker slipped from her lips. Chickadee continued to beller and squeal.

All of a sudden I heard the thundering of hooves. I knew it was not Goldie or Barbie.

They were watching from the distance. Out of the corner of my eye I saw it. A black and white milk cow had scurried from the field. She came to save Chickadee. This was Lulu. Lulu already had three calves. She felt the need to protect Chickadee.

Lulu surprised Chickadee so much, the fighting stopped. Lulu put her black, wet nose to Chickadee's. Chickadee's brown eyes opened wide. Her eyes opened even wider when Lulu started licking her. A cow does

this when they are taking care of their babies. Chickadee winced as the long, slobbery tongue glided over her cheek. Chick watched with amazement. Barbie, Goldie and I did, too!

Lulu, Chickadee's adopted mother, finally left. Everything settled down. Chickadee did not fight me anymore. She followed me like a puppy. Goldie, Barbie, Chick, Lulu and her babies all went to grazing, or eating.

I thought this was the end of the cow situation. Was I ever wrong!

A few days later everyone was in the field grazing. Being the Spring of the year, flowers were just showing their faces. The tiny green hands of trees joyfully waved hello. Newborn animals of all sorts could be seen. Baby bunnies hopped here and there. Tiny ducklings followed their mom to the nearby Sun River.

I noticed something beside Chick. I knew it was not spry Chickadee. She continued to romp and play. I had to go see.

The closer I got, the more amazed I was. There, next to Chick, nursing, or drinking milk from her was a little black and white calf. It was one of Lulu's. Lulu watched angrily. Chick did not mind at all. She was happy to be a mother. When the calf was done eating, Chickadee stepped in for lunch. Once full, she continued her job of playing.

Chickadee was always so playful and rambunctious I worried about breaking her to ride.

I was in for a surprise!

4
THE LESSON

When Chickadee was two, it was time to break her. To break a horse means to train it to be ridden. Her reaction to being halter broke put fear into me! What a fight she put up. I kept thinking of her bucking in my arms. How could I stay on if she bucked like that while I was riding her!

Saddling Chickadee the first time was scary. I tied her up good. I always used a bowline knot on a young, green horse. You can loosen this special knot if the horse pulls back or jerks backwards. A green horse is one that has not been ridden very many times. They might get scared and pull tight on the knot.

Toting the saddle pad, I eased up to Chickadee. She watched out of the corner of her eye. I was preparing for a big explosion. I gently slid the thick pad onto her. The pad goes underneath the saddle. This protects the horse's back. Chickadee's muscles tensed up. I stood very still, waiting. Then….she relaxed. A big sigh rushed from her flared nostrils. What a relief!

Now came the saddle. Chickadee was hardly bothered by my walking up to her with the saddle. I used the same saddle I had gotten new when I was breaking Chick. I gently set the saddle on Chickadee's back. Then I slowly tightened the cinch. The cinch holds the saddle on the horse's back. I only tightened the cinch a little at first. I only got it snug. Every few minutes I tightened it more. The cinch needs to be tight enough to hold the saddle in place when you are sitting in it.

If you fully tighten the cinch on a young horse too quickly, the horse is more prone to buck. Tightening it too quickly can also make a horse 'cinchy'. This is when the horse is very touchy about the cinch. If a horse is cinchy, it might pull back when it is tied up. The horse might start running backwards as fast as it can go. A cinchy horse sometimes will stretch out its body and not budge. A really bad thing a cinchy horse does is flip over backwards. You do not want to ruin the young horse. This is why I took my time cinching Chickadee up.

Chickadee did not mind being saddled. She stood quietly. This was quite a shock to me! She was great putting the bridle on, too. She took the bit right into her mouth. I wondered if she was trying to trick me. She was making me think she would not buck when I rode her.

I wanted to saddle Chickadee up several times before I got on her. I figured that would at least get her used to the saddle. This is what I wanted to do with Barbie, too. Chickadee saddled up just like Barbie.

Chickadee acted great this first time with the saddle and bridle on. The warm Spring sun settled on us. There was no breeze to blow the dust. Fresh flowers sent their scent our way. Without even thinking, I put my foot in the stirrup and stepped right on Chickadee. When I realized what I had done, I about died. Panic filled me. I then remembered my father telling me a horse always senses when you are scared. If the horse thinks you are scared, it is more likely to act up. I relaxed.

Chickadee started walking around the corral. Like with Goldie, she acted like she was already broke. Her walk was amazing. Many times when a horse is first ridden, they do not like to walk with ease. Chickadee walked right out. Like when I first saw her, she walked extremely fast.

Although Chickadee was acting broke in the corral, she had a shock coming outside!

5
THE SCARE

Right away I started riding Chickadee outside the round corral. She did fantastic. She was so much fun to ride. She strutted with that wonderful fast walk she had. She did everything just right. She was so friendly and great to catch and saddle. She was quite a joy.

Chick, Goldie and Barbie always watched as we went for our rides. They seemed to be a bit jealous.

Chick never did like me riding other horses but her. I guess her two daughters were taking after her!

Chickadee did most everything right. She did one bad thing other young horses do, though. She would not walk in a straight line. Crossing a big open pasture took forever. Rather than walk straight, she zig-zagged. If her tail had ink on it, a trail of Z's would have been left across the field. It was as though she wanted to mark the varied colors of wild flowers.

It takes a young horse quite a few rides before they will walk straight. You have to keep turning them back to keep them straight.

The horse finally figures out you do not want it to zig-zag.

Walking straight is one thing a young horse has to learn. It also has to get accustomed to different types of animals it encounters. Chick, Barbie and Goldie all had to get used to rabbits jumping in front of them. The beautiful Chinese pheasant shooting like a missile into the air past their noses shocked them. Worse yet, the ominous rattlesnake coiling between their legs frightened them!

Once Chickadee and I were zig-ging and zagging on a hillside. There was still snow in some spots. Dots of blue, red and yellow blossoms peeked at us from other areas. Soft, white clouds left from the chilly morning were resting on the tips of the mountains.

Chickadee was already familiarized with rabbits, snakes and birds. All of a sudden the silent air was filled with a shrill squeal. Chickadee's furry ears went straight up. Just a few feet from us, standing tall from its home in the cold, hard ground, was a badger. It was like a concrete statue.

A badger is a gray, furry mammal with a black and white head. Its face is in the shape of a triangle. Its beady eyes are black. The pointed nose has long whiskers shooting from it. The badger is also very ferocious. It is a larger version of a gopher.

Chickadee stopped fast in her tracks. Her soft ears pointed toward the badger. Her body tensed.

I did not have to steer Chickadee hard to get her to veer around the badger. She realized we needed to stay at a safe distance. The badger watched as we slipped into the distance. Knowing he was safe, he dropped like a falling rock down to his protected home.

Chickadee did well with the badger, but she was about to meet bigger, scarier animals!

6

THE TRIP

The time came for Chickadee to take the same trip her sisters Barbie and Goldie had taken. This was the trip into the mountains to look for elk. An elk is of the deer family but very large. It also has very large antlers. An antler is a tall, bony structure on each side of the animal's head. They are like horns on a bull. Like with deer, the elk's antlers fall off every spring. New antlers then grow back, bigger than the previous year. Horns on an animal are different than antlers. They do not fall off, or shed, every year.

This trip was going to be very special. All three sisters were going. I was very excited to see how they would do. I knew Barbie and Goldie would do fine. They had already taken the trip.

The ride into camp was breathtaking. It was along the same little creek (rhymes with stick in Montana) Goldie had jumped. Barbie and I had listened to its continual hum. Chickadee was mesmerized watching the cool water. It rumbled over the rounded rocks in perfect rhythm with distant crickets.

Tall, slender pine trees sent their aroma through the air. We almost saw the smell of the trees. It was so strong. Tiny chipmunks scurried back and forth from their tall castles.

By the time we got into camp, all three sisters were happy to be there. They were ready to rest. The hitching post looked like a bed to them. This is where they would be tied at night.

I was concerned about the three being tied up. I remembered what had happened to Barbie. A mean horse next to her kicked and hurt her. That is why I had to ride Goldie when she was yet green.

That night I hardly slept. I listened to the creek whispering across its hard bed. Owls sang their songs. Sometimes a lone coyote played harmony. I was waiting for the sound of the commotion of hooves like before. Protecting my face from the brisk, mountain air, I dozed. Before I knew it, it was time to get up. The sun rising did not wake me. It was still dark. The slight whinny from Barbie told me it was time for her breakfast. Chickadee chimed in, agreeing with her.

As soon as I realized I was awake, I jumped out of my sleeping bag. I darted straight to the girls to make sure no one was hurt. To my relief, they were all fine. The ground's frost on my feet told me to get my boots on!

Once saddled, we went looking for the secretive elk. The stars slyly winked at us. Every so often one shot through the darkness like an arrow. Slivers of the full-moon's rays slipped through the trees' slender branches.

The elk ate through the night. Sometimes we caught them still eating very early in the day. Later in the morning and through the day, they lay intertwined in the thick trees. Their coarse coats blended in with the brush and branches. We had to look closely to ever see one. Sometimes we rode right by them without even knowing they were there.

This trip was very nice. We were able to see many elk. Since Barbie was so frightened of ‘odd’ animals, she stayed back at camp. I was worried about how Chickadee would react when she saw the majestic animal. I remembered how Barbie acted! They were full sisters. I thought they might act the same.

The elk did not bother Chickadee at all. With her ears pointed forward, she watched them both eating and sleeping. When the cow elk, or mothers, looked toward us, Chickadee seemed to know to stand still. The cows' calves, or baby elk, continued eating. They knew their moms took care of them.

Chickadee had quite an adventure on her next trip!

7

THE TADPOLE

Another nice trip we took was into the mountains near Lincoln, Montana. This was an area near the Scapegoat Wilderness. There were many elk here, too. We ended up riding on old logging roads. These roads were used by trucks to haul trees out of the mountains.

It was in July. While it was extremely hot down lower, the high mountains provided a cooler climate. Chickadee enjoyed riding these roads. Spunky chipmunks scurried in front of us. They did not bother her. Black crows threw their "Caw, caw" at us. We were trespassing on their land.

The trees were thick where we rode. One spot opened into a beautiful pond. Chickadee enjoyed drinking the cool water out of it. Her head was bent close to the water. Looking past her pointed ears, I saw something. I had to get off her to see. Standing, I looked into the crystal-clear water. Little black dots scuttled here and there. A closer look was needed.

I laid on my stomach. Chickadee

wondered what I was doing. With my face almost touching the water, I saw. The water was only about six inches deep all across the pond. Millions of tadpoles scooted here and there. A tadpole is a young toad that is in the larva stage. It lives in water. Like fish, it breathes through gills. On its dot of a body is a long tail. No legs have formed yet.

I had never seen so many tadpoles. There were as many as the grains of sand around the pond. Many frogs would be living there when the tadpoles grew up!

The minute tadpoles darted every which way. Chickadee's head snapped back and forth trying to keep up with them. I did not try.

Chickadee and I finally got tired of watching the flighty amphibian. The warm sun was setting. We had to head home. The picture of the fascinating tadpoles stayed in my head.

Chickadee and I went on many nice trips together. We were able to see the varied wildlife. There was always a new kind of bird flying above us. My favorite was the magnificent bald eagle. Its pure white tail and head remained spotless against a dark sky.

Although Chickadee enjoyed these trips, she had a job to do!

8

THE ARENA

Chickadee was a wonderful horse to ride in the mountains. She rode well on the flat, too. Her walk was very fast and smooth. This made her fun to ride. She became inured with things around her like animals and trees.

Chickadee also needed to learn to be a working cow horse. This is one that can be used to gather, work and rope cattle.

One way Chickadee was trained to be a cow horse was to start right off gathering cattle. This is just what her sisters and mom did.

I started riding Chickadee in the smaller corral. As soon as the cattle needed to be gathered, we went and did it.

Chickadee did not neck rein yet. I pulled her nose in the direction I wanted her to go. When I did this, the rein touched the opposite side of her neck. The rein is a strap of leather. It is attached to the bit. The bit is in the horse's mouth. It is used to control the horse. In time, Chickadee learned when the rein touched her neck, she was to turn away from it.

Chickadee and I also spent a lot of time in the roping arena. Here we ‘tracked’ critters. This meant we followed a calf or steer. A calf is a baby cow. A steer is the male of the cattle family. It cannot be a father.

Like the hands of a clock, round and round the arena we rode. If the critter slowed down, we did. If it ran faster, we did. If there was no breeze, we ate the critter's dust. Dust does not taste good. A slight breeze swept the dust away, leaving fresh air to breathe and smell.

Sometimes I swung my rope while we were tracking. This got Chickadee used to the rope. There might come a time when we had to rope a calf to brand it. When calves or cows are sick, they need to be roped to doctor them, or take care of them.

After constant tracking, Chickadee learned to stay right on the calf. She kept her nose on the critter's

back no matter which way it ran. That way, when I went to rope on her, she always had me sitting in a position to catch the calf. If I had to rope a critter outside the arena, she always had me right where I needed to be.

Chickadee, like Barbie, Goldie, Chick and Dan, was cowy. This meant she enjoyed chasing cows.

If a calf turned back toward us, Chickadee worked like a cutting horse. She looked the calf in the eyes. Every time the quick-moving calf jumped one way, Chickadee did the same. Back and forth we went. Dan did this in competitions.

Chickadee learned to track a critter very well. That quality and her fast walk made her a wonderful working horse.

This is why I was so sad with what happened next.

For

9

THE SAD DAY

Chickadee was one of the most fun horses I had ever ridden. She traveled across the country faster than any horse we were with. They trotted to keep up.

Chickadee was friendly and loving. She thoroughly loved me riding her. We had many wonderful times together. She was also beautiful. This is why everyone wanted to buy her.

There was one particular lady that loved Chickadee as much as I did. Every time she saw Chickadee, she asked if she could buy her.

I was riding Chickadee one beautiful Spring day. The sun was begging the flowers to come to life. The air held nothing but freshness in it. A pickup towing a horse trailer pulled up to us. It was the same lady. She had been watching Chickadee's fancy, fast walk. Chickadee's body had turned from a pitch black to a frosted black. Her muscles moved with every move she made. Her gentle eyes watched everything.

The lady asked again if I would sell Chickadee. Since I had too many horses, I hesitantly said yes. I would sell her Chickadee. As soon as I said it, my heart sank. I felt like it was in my stomach. I was filled with disbelief. How could I get rid of Chickadee?

I looked at Barbie and Goldie. My eyes filled with tears as they threw me their loving glances. I had to look away. I could not look into Chickadee's dark eyes.

I slowly and sadly walked Chickadee to the barn. I could only look at the ground in front of me. The lady stayed right with us. Pulling Chickadee's saddle off, I told her I was sorry. I could not say it very loudly. My voice was choking from the sadness.

Loading into the trailer, Chickadee looked over her shoulder at me. She looked so confused. She looked at Barbie and Goldie. They whinnied. They knew she was leaving.

I tried to tell myself it was okay. Chickadee would have a good home. She would be living at the base of the Highwood Mountains. The closest town was little Geyser, Montana.

I did not convince myself that everything would be fine. They pulled away. I heard Chickadee's last whinny. I broke down. I could not hold back the tears.

Chickadee was always on my

mind. I relived all of our rides. Barbie and Goldie seemed to always look for her. I missed her so much. I ached. So did they.

A few weeks later, the lady called me on the telephone. When I heard her voice, I knew something had happened to Chickadee. I was trembling with fear. The more she talked, the happier I was. She could not keep Chickadee. She wondered if I would like her back. How could I say no?!

Once Chickadee was back with us, our happy family was complete again. Our joyful rides continued.

If they could have talked, I know Barbie, Goldie and Chick would have all thanked me for bringing Chickadee back to us!

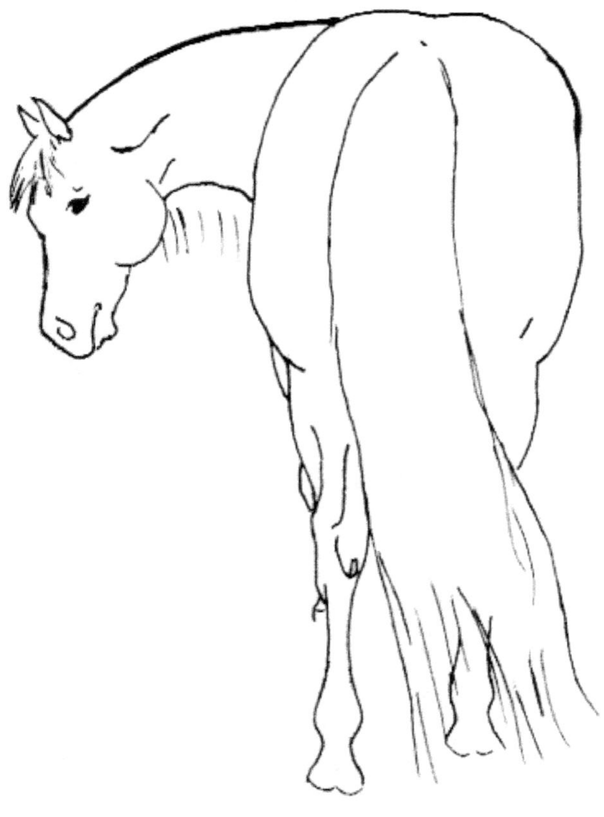

10

THE FAMILY

The bond between family members is one that should never be cut. Chick, Barbie, Goldie and Chickadee always had that bond. It was evident. They always stood together. Played together. Talked to each other. When one was not with the four, they looked for the absent one.

The same should always be with humans or any animals. Nothing should ever come between family members. No matter if they were apart for a while, Chick, Barbie, Goldie and Chickadee still showed the same love for each other when they were reunited. It was obvious they were family.

I was very fortunate to have experienced this love. I knew they all loved me. I loved them just as much. I almost felt that I was part of their family.

I now see Chick's grandchildren and great-grandchildren. From generation to generation, they all still love me. I see Chick in them all and see the love they have for each other. I see Chickadee in Belle. They look and ride the same.

Chickadee will always be in my heart. Memories of our times together go on forever. I thank her for all of them! She was beautiful. She was kind. She traveled the country quickly! I am so happy I was able to get to know her.

ZC HORSES SERIES

Now that you have met Chick and some of her children, you will get to meet one of their companions. You will finally meet Darby. You have heard about him in some of the previous stories. You will be amazed by things that happenned to him. You will fall in love with him when you learn of his personality. You will be amazed when you hear the terrible thing someone did to him. You will smile reading the 9th in the **'ZC HORSES'** series, ***"Darby-The Cow Dog"***.

Be sure to be there to greet him!!

ZC HORSES SERIES #9
Darby-The Cow Dog

by Diane W. Keaster

Coming October 2004

Order Form

ZC HORSES SERIES

Don't miss out on any part of the lives of Chick and her many babies and friends! Experience all of the rides, joys and sorrows. Don't be left out!

___	Chick-The Beginning! (Spring 2001)	$7.95
___	Chick-The Saddle Horse! (September 2001)	$7.95
___	Chick-The Mom! (April 2002)	$7.95
___	Luke-The First! (September 2002)	$7.95
___	Barbie-The Best! (Oct. 2002)	$7.95
___	Leroy-The Stallion! (September 2003)	$7.95
___	Goldie-The Wise! (March 2004)	$7.95
___	Chickadee-The Traveler! (September 2004)	$7.95
___	Darby-The Cow Dog! (October 2004)	$7.95
___	Sonny-The Spectacular! (December 2004)	$7.95

UPCOMING TITLES

Tawny-The Beauty!	Apple-The Joy!
Onie-The Roanie!	Belle-The Sweetie!
Classy-The Special!	Lily-The Pretty Paint!
Black Jack-The Great !	Slick-TheFriend!

Also read about Cider, Buck, Nellie, Junie, Eagle, Smokey, Sarge, Tex, Radar and many more!

ZC HORSES SERIES, 8 Hokanson Ln, Salmon, ID 83467
(208) 756-7947
www.zchorses.com
Email: zchorses@hotmail.com

Please send me the books I have checked above. I am enclosing US $____(please add $2/bk to cover shipping and handling). Send check or money order, please.

NAME________________________________

ADDRESS_____________________________

CITY/STATE/ZIP_________________________

PHONE_______________________________

To My Reader:

I was born and raised on a ranch near a little town called Belt, Montana. After receiving my B.S. in Business Education from Montana State University, I taught high school business. I then moved on to other facets of employment.

The whole time, I was team roping and raising, breaking and training horses. The profession I fell into by mistake was trading horses. Throughout my life, I have handled hundreds of horses, all which have a story of their own.

My sons, Cole and Augustus, loved reading stories about horses when they were small and I loved reading the stories to them. That is why I am writing these books. I want to tell the stories of the creatures I love to the children I love.

My sons and husband Chuck and I all have moved to a new home in Salmon on the Lemhi River which runs into the beautiful Salmon River. We are close to the Continental Divide. All of our wonderful companions have come with us and love their new home!

I thank Jehovah our Creator for giving us such a wonderful, beautiful animal!

Enjoy the stories!

NOTES AND PICTURES!!!!

NOTES AND PICTURES!!!!

NOTES AND PICTURES!!!!

NOTES AND PICTURES!!!!

NOTES AND PICTURES!!!!

NOTES AND PICTURES!!!!

NOTES AND PICTURES!!!!

NOTES AND PICTURES!!!!

NOTES AND PICTURES!!!!

NOTES AND PICTURES!!!!

NOTES AND PICTURES!!!!

NOTES AND PICTURES!!!!

www.ingramcontent.com/pod-product-compliance
Lightning Source LLC
LaVergne TN
LVHW020649100826
845148LV00012B/2405

* 9 7 8 0 9 7 2 1 4 9 6 7 9 *